Katharina Eder

"The Color Purple" by Alice Walker - an Analysis

Katharina Eder

"The Color Purple" by Alice Walker - an Analysis

GRIN Verlag

Bibliografische Information der Deutschen Nationalbibliothek: Die Deutsche Bibliothek
verzeichnet diese Publikation in der Deutschen Nationalbibliografie; detaillierte bibliografische Daten sind im Internet über http://dnb.d-nb.de/ abrufbar.

1. Auflage 2007
Copyright © 2007 GRIN Verlag
http://www.grin.com/
Druck und Bindung: Books on Demand GmbH, Norderstedt Germany
ISBN 978-3-640-91532-3

The color purple

Alice Walker

Katharina Eder

WS 07/08

Universität Wien

Table of content

1. Introduction

The Color Purple is Alice Walker's masterpiece, which made the author not only the first female Afro American author to receive a Pulitzer Price but moreover brought her world fame and a broader recognition of her other works. This analysis of the text focuses on motifs, themes and symbolism used in the story. It also talks about the author by giving an in-dept overview not only about her life but also the sociocultural background that shaped this novel. As mentioned before a clear focus is put on themes, symbols and motifs in the novel, which are widely used and therefore also are somehow responsible for the diversity of approaches to reading the novel. The textual analysis is enhanced by a brief summary of the plot, characters and their relationship as well as a compressed paragraph talking about the setting and an overview over some narrative techniques used in the novel.

2. Biography

> Alice (Malsenior) Tallulah-Kate Walker, American by nationality and
> African American, Cherokee and Scottish-Irish by ethnicity, is a southern
> writer. (Bates 23)

Alice Walker was born in Eatonton, Georgia, in February 1944 as the youngest of 8 siblings. She did not have to support her family on the field, where they worked as sharecroppers, a job that Walker considered as even worse than the subjugation of slavery. (see Bates 8) At the age of 8 Walker joined her brothers in a game of cowboys and Indians, where she was accidentally shot in the right eye by one of them. This incident was particularly significant for the writer. First an active child, Walker retrenched now from active life, and felt depressive. Walker's educational life had started at the age of 4. An outstanding student, Walker, attended Spellman College as well as Sarah Lawrence, where she graduated in 1965. While still at college Walker also started traveling. Her first journeys brought her to Africa, and Europe. From there she returned with new impressions that inspired her writing. In writing Walker was also strongly influenced by her two sisters Ruth and Molly. While Ruth escaped as soon as possible, from their home and the suppression of their verbally violent father, Molly got a scholarship, went to college and traveled independently around the world. As different as both life stories might sound, both sisters provided Walker with stories about life, that influenced the writers later works. (see Bates 1-15) It was Ruth who talked with Alice about the lover's triangle which both had heard of, a story that should give Alice the inspiration for the Color Purple, having first the characters of Celie and Shug in mind. (see In Search 355)

Supporting the Civil Right Movement Walker met her later husband, Melvyn R. Leventhal a Civil Right lawyer who she married in 1967 and had her daughter Rebeca with. Married to a white, Jew, Walker speaks about the racial segregation of the United States as the *American Apartheid*, cumulating in the Civil Right Movement. Walker and her husband were the first interracial married couple in Mississippi, a state that only started allowing interracial relationships from the year 1967 onwards. Before that it was illegal to be in an interracial relationship not only in Mississippi, 16 other states forbade relationships between different races up to the year 1966. However, Walker's marriage, although full of love and admiration, which can clearly be seen in her text *Beloved* published in her book *The Way Forward is with a Broken Heart* (2001), was not meant to last. The couple divorced in 1976.

Walker was a gifted writer from the start. She won prizes and scholarships. Her debut novel was *The Third Life of Grange Copeland* (1970), poems, short stories and novels followed. Among them *In Love and Trouble: Stories of Black Women* (1973), *Meridian* (1976) and *You Can't keep a Good Woman Down* (1981). In 1982 *The Color Purple*, so far Walkers most successful book, was published. In 1985 it was made into a film by Steven Spielberg. A 2005 musical version, produced by Oprah Winfrey, which opened on the Broadway and also toured through America, followed. As the greatest success, however, the book itself can be considered. It won a Pulitzer Prize and made Walker the first African American to achieve the prestige carrying price. Besides writing Alice Walker has been teaching at different Colleges and Universities, Wellesly College and Yale University are only two of them.

Her private life always had a great impact on Walkers texts and thoughts. Due to this fact it needs to be mentioned that Walker relationship with women have sometimes been ambiguous. Women seem to have dominated Walkers life so far. The writer adored her mother and has, from an early age on, been interested in female writers and later started to ground "her work in a matrilinieal tradition of black writing." (Walker

Preface ix) Walker also loves her daughter Rebeca but she had problems in managing her career and her motherhood as she confesses in her story *A Writer Because of, Nor in Spite of, Her Children* published in *In Search of Our Mother's Gardens* (1983). Besides heterosexual love ties, Walker also had female partners who she referred to as lovers.

3. Sociocultural Background

Although slavery was prohibited by the Emancipation Proclamation of the year 1862, Blacks were still not included in everyday life. They were hardly able to find well payed jobs or work at all. While some had the chance to open small businesses of their own, mainly selling dry goods, others had to continuou or start working on fields. Working on fields meant working as "sharecroppers, tenant farmers, farm laborers, and casuals (work for food)". (Bates 91) By the end of the 18th century and during the 19th century, however, farmer were given the opportunity to buy their own land and tools to start their own businesses. Walker places *The Color Purple* in the American South among independent but still poor farmers. (see Bates 91)

"Walker's heritage and history provides a vehicle for understanding the modern world in which her characters live." (Davis 26) Her heritage and the modern society she grew up in are of utmost importance to understand the novel. Walker included herself strongly in the Civil Right Movement, which was not always easy at this time. Was being black already difficult enough at this time, meant being a woman another challenge. Although there was the fight for equal rights, in the beginning, it did not include necessarily female rights. (see Joannau 192) Thus Walker can be seen as a southern, black feminist or using the author's words *womanist*.

4. Textual Analysis

4.1. Plot

At the beginning of the story the reader learns, how Celie, then a 14 year old girl is raped by her, then thought to be father. The two children conceived by him are given away. Later Celie herself is given away into marriage, to Mr. ___, that is also full of abuse. Celie who fears that her sister Nettie could also be raped by their "father", asks her sister to stay with them but Mr. ___, who was interested in Nettie even before his marriage to Celie, tries to start a sexual relationship with her. This makes Nettie run away, she joins a family of missionaries and follows them to Africa. (see Bobo 62-65)

Meanwhile Celie's stepson Harpo marries the strong, black Sofia. Harpo wants to follow his father's and Celie's example of marriage and starts beating Sofia, who as she had to fight most of the men in her family before, fights back but is finally so exasperated and crestfallen that she leaves him.

One day Mr. ___ brings home his lover, Shug, who is first skeptical and even harsh with Celie. The relationship, however, changes after Celie nourished the sick Shug. A very close and strong friendship develops that leads not only to a sexual relationship but to a deep love between the two women. Meanwhile Sofia is sent to prison because she fought the major after his wife had asked her to be her maid. Sofia's strength to survive in prison, her courage and Shug's love encourage Celie to stand up to Mr. ___. Celie's *revolution* is also supported by Nettie's letters to her, that Shug found hidden in Mr. ___ property. The letters tell Celie that not only her beloved sister but also her children are still alive. (see Bobo 64-65) In the end of the story the reader finds a transformed Mr. ___, who learned to do housework on his own and a freed Celie. A reunion of Celie with her children and Nettie forms the conciliatory end.

4.2. Characters and their relationship

Celie is introduced to the reader through her confession that she is raped by her father, later to be known as her stepfather, Alphonso. Celie is a girl of 14 at this time, she has not found her inner strength when she is sexually abused for the first time, she denies herself "out of misplaced loyalty to black men or adherence to societal codes that dictate confining gender roles" (Winchell ix). A fact that can be seen in her obedience to Alphonso who also silences her by the threat that a revealing would kill her mother. Her later marriage with Albert is marked by the same concept of obedience that seems only to be broken when she meets Shug, who encourages Celie to start a life of her own. First still obeying, even to Shug, Celie is later on able to reveal her physical abuse by Mr. _____ to her lover. The singer is shocked and promises not to leave her until "Albert won't even think about beating" (Purple 72) her again. It is this bond between Celie and Shug and the coincidence that Shug finds Nettie's letters that help Celie to find happiness in life.

Celie's sister Nettie is spared the sexual abuse due to her sister's altruistic sacrifice. When Alphonso lays his eyes on Nettie for the first time, Celie promises herself to prevent her sister from a similar dreadful destiny. (see Purple 5) Moreover Nettie has the chance of education which is denied to Celie as soon as she is pregnant for the first time. However Nettie shares her knowledge with Celie which helps the latter to develop the ability of reading and writing. Albert is unable to live the life he wanted to. Still in love with Shug he marries Celie, to have somebody to take care of his children. It is his inability to live according to his dreams that makes him beat Celie. (see Purple 71)

"Shug's boldness is her asset." (Bates 98) Shug is a wild, strong, independent character, she does not adept to any of the cliché role models of the time, although Bates describes her as a "transformed southern belle" (Bates 97). She is active and independent in ways of thinking and living. Her children live with her mother so that she can devote her life to music. Like Shug, Sofia is a strong independent woman who always had to fight to avoid oppression. (see Purple 39) When Harpo starts beating her, she fights back, just like she fought the men in her family before. However, Sofia's fight for independence is not rewarded, she gets send to prison for a fight with a white man and is battered beyond recognition.

Harpo and Sofia could have the most beautiful relationship. They seem to complete one another. While Harpo likes working in the household Sofia likes to work outdoors, she repairs the roof, she timbers a swing for the porch. Nonetheless Harpo's inability to neglect the well-established gender roles is the reason for the end of their marriage.

4.3. Motifs/Themes/Symbolism
4.3.1. Motifs
One of the themes most present are letters, as mentioned earlier the novel is an epistolary novel, which means it is written in letters. Writing in general has an immense power. In *The Color Purple* it helps the protagonist Celie to overcome abuse by writing letters to god. She gains freedom through writing and is voicing her inflicted silence by addressing them to god. Those letters also help her to start communication with other's. (see Collins 202) Letters are also used by Nettie to free herself. She writes about her thoughts, her dreams, her wishes, never giving up, although severely doubting in the end, the hope to get a letter back. Her letters are of the utmost importance to Celie. Once they are found by Shug they give Celie strength, happiness and generally speaking alleviation. The last letter in the book is addressed not only to god but also the stars,

trees and many more. It is letter full of gratitude. (see Purple 259)

4.3.2. Themes
4.3.2.1. Violence
Violence is one of the central themes of the novel. Although only mentioned in the end , the lynching of Celie's father, can be considered the actual start of the story. He is among two men, lynched by white men who are jealous of his business. Nettie is the one who brings this revelation, which shocks Celie.

> My daddy lynch. My mama crazy. All my little half-brothers and sisters no
> kin to me. My children not my sister and brother. Pa not my pa. (Purple 160)

Racial violence is however not the center of the novel which mainly talks about physical violence and rape mainly in a black community. One might however argue it finally succeeds sexual abuse. (see Berlant 216) For using violence as a central topic, Walker was also influenced by the community of Eatonton, the town she grew up in. The rate of domestic violence as well as the rate of rape and sexual violence was according to Walker high. (see Joannou 176). In the story violence seems to be bequeathed between the generations. Harpo and his father, as well as his grandfather, all use violence in their relationship. Although Harpo finds it hard to beat Sofia, he finally gives in to the cultural pressure. (see Bates 97) "Race, class violence are a result of societal influence". (Bates 97) Furthermore the author argues that Walker demonstrates the refusal of the South to relinquish the power it once had over human beings.

4.3.2.2. Female narrative voice
At the beginning of the novel, although silenced by violence, Celie is still able to regain her voice by writing letters to god and in consequence opening up to other people, gaining a stronger and stronger female narrative voice over the years, allowing the reader to hear about a story, influenced by the black history of the South, from a female standpoint. (see Bates 96)

4.3.2.3. Female relationships
Walker *The Color Purple* is a celebration of female friendship and relationship. Black literature in general often avers the importance of female relationship, Walker stresses

that once more. (Collins 104) Walker's women help each other, set examples for another and, although they often are at a variance, form strong unions. The most significant relationship thereby seems to be Celie's bond with Nettie and her bond with her mother who she dares not to "kill" by telling her about her rape. Sofia's bond with her sisters that she sees as the "source of her feistiness" (Bates 97) as well as Shug's and Celie's relationship could also be considered of an utmost relevance. As mentioned earlies those bonds also show through action. Celie's children are raised by Nettie, Shug promises not to leave Celie until she is sure Mr. ___ won't hit her anymore. (see Purple 52) Nevertheless the most important action of all is Celie's sacrifice of herself to prevent her sister from any harm (see Bates 100-101)

The quilt Sofia and Celie work on after Celie's betrayal and their falling out, can be seen as a symbol of female relationship and will be discussed in detail later. In general female bonds of friendship manifest themselves in shared work. (see Johnson 108)

4.3.2.4. Identity

Celie portraits herself by telling her sexual history. Yet Rosalina Coward warns in an essay "against the reproduction of an ideology where female identity is constructed solely in relationship to sexuality" (Hooks 285). She also warns that women should not only get to know themselves by sexual exploitation. Walker on the other side uses sexuality in *The Color Purple* as a powerful instrument that can "subvert oppressive structures" (Hooks 285)

Walker portrays some of her female characters as women that had not found their strength yet. (see Winchell ix) Especially *The Color Purple* illustrates the change of the protagonist from an invisible woman to a secure, mature woman. At this Walker's male characters should not be forgotten, they are also given the possibility of growth and transformation like Mr. ___ who at the end of the novel even learns to do the housekeeping for himself.

> The first thing I notice about Mr. ___ is how clean he is. His skin shine. His hair brush back. [...] He out here in the field from sunup to sundown. And clean that house just like a woman. Even cook, say Harpo. And what more, wash the dishes when he finish. (Purple 201)

4.3.2.5. Sexuality

"The Color Purple is a narrative of 'sexual confession.'" (Hooks 284) undermined by the fact that the reader learns about Celie through her "sexual history", which is presented in an open and quite graphical way.

> First he put his thing up against my hip and sort of wiggle it around. Then he grabs hold of my titties. Then he put his thing inside my pussy. (Purple 3)

It is through sexual discovery of her own body that Celie learns to accept her body, identities areas she did not even know about and finally achieves pleasure through sex, something that she so far only had associated with pain. Shug's and Celie's relationship stands for the paradigm of homo-erotic affairs between women. A homosexual relationship is, men and women equally denied but when it comes to sexuality, men even encourage sexuality between women as pornographic fiction undermines. (see Hooks 286) Walker's aim however cannot be seen as part of this category. Moreover she wants to "'arouse disgust, outrage, and anger of male sexual exploitation of females". (Hooks 286) A fact that Walker emphasizes by pointing out that black women often functioned as "outlet" for misuse by men. They functioned as breeders, raping them for pleasure was common at a time. (see Collins 135) The myth that "all" black men are rapists, according to Davis (see Collins 147), is thereby in close connection with the myth of black women being whores.

Celie whose sexuality is owned by men is finally, although helped by Shug able to explore and free her sexuality.

> She say, Here, take this mirror, and go look at yourself down there, I bet you never seen it, have you? [...] Stick the looking glass tween my legs. Ugh. All that hair. Then my pussy lips be black. Then inside look like a wet rose. It a lot prettier than you thought, ain't it? She say from the door. It mine, I say. (Purple 67-68)

4.3.3. Symbolism
4.3.3.1. Purple

When Mr. _____'s sisters visit they advice him to buy Celie a new dress. Celie is fond of the idea and starts thinking which color the dress should have. "I think what color Shug Avery would wear. She like a queen to me so I say to Kate, somethin purple, maybe a little red in it too." (Purple, 21) Celie associates the color purple with royalty and Walker herself refers to the color purple as "color that is always a surprise but is every where in nature" (Purple ix). Considering both references one might argue that Walker wanted to find Celie her own purple, her own royalty which everyone inherits but first might not be aware of. During the book Celie develops from a suppressed to a highly independent woman and blossoms like a flower, considering the authors statement a purple one.

The color purple seems to be of utmost importance to Alice Walker as she uses it considerably often in her other stories and texts. The author who created the term womanist, to refer to a black feminist, uses purple for example to stress the importance to have a different term then feminist by saying "womanist is to feminist like purple to lavender" (see In Search xi-xii). Arguable is whether purple and lavender are used to refer to skin tones, white referring to lavender, black to purple, or whether Walker used the more intense color to underline its standing to shine out the "feminine" lavender, reminding the reader of the importance of being a feminist. Feminism which grew paler and paler through the last years should gain energy again and therefore presume a stronger color, purple.

As mentioned before Walker uses the color purple in a large number of stories. Among them *The Child Who Favored Daughter* where she uses the color to refer to a black man who is blushing: "the red underneath his skin glowing purple". (In Love & Trouble 41) In *The Color Purple*, where so many men (and women) could blush according to their acts, this metaphor however is regrettably not used.

4.3.3.2. God

The Color Purple is an epistolary novel, in the form of letters first written by Celie to god and later on from Nettie to Celie and vica versa. God plays a very prominent role through out the novel. God is Celie's only friend over a long time, she considers him a friend, when she tells him that she is a 14 year old girl, she introduces herself to him in the same manner as someone would address people she is introduced to. God is Celie's only confident, sharing with her the dark secret of her rape and child bearing

11

experiences, as her stepfather has limited her in speaking about her problem by telling her that if she talked about it, "it would kill your mammy". (Purple 3) A quite ironical situation is created when Squeak returns from helping Sofia. She was raped at the Sheriffs office and does not want to tell the others about it. Shug however tries to make her speak by asking "Who you gon tell, god?" (Purple 90) Basically exact the thing Celie did.

In *The Color Purple* the church functions as a symbol for God. Celie's god is a stereotypical god. She describes him as white, looking like a banker. Celie thinks he is almighty a fact that becomes even more obvious when she describes how god safes Sofia by blowing "out a big breath of fire" (Purple 97) to suddenly free the captured Sofia. Throughout the novel, Celie's perception of God changes thanks to Shug who "assures her that god loves sex, and that god is not white but is in everything." (Johnson 94)

Yvonne Johnson refers to Walker as being "obsessed with spirituality" and indeed "the spirit" is of utmost importance at the beginning as well as the end of the novel where Walker thanks "the spirit" for coming. (see Johnson 108)

4.3.3.3. Sewing and Trousers
When Alice Walker graduated from college, she was the best in her class and was therefore given a large number of presents. Among them a sewing machine, her mother, who did not earn much, less than 20 Dollars a week, gave her. Her mother's generosity made Walker cherish this present even more. (see In Search) The reason why Walker's mother had given her this present was that she wanted her daughter to be independent in making her own cloth, as this was considered as a sign of liberty, which shows in a great number of Walker's novels. In *The Color Purple* Celie liberates her self by starting to sew pants, first encouraged by Shug Avery, Celie soon learns the real value of her pants, which soon become so popular that Celie could even start her own shop. Sewing not only supports Celie with the money she needs to be independent but it also frees her in her thinking, with the help of Shug Avery she dares to break the taboo of women wearing trousers.

Sewing is one way for women to begin the process of self-reclamation because it represents, more than other activities traditionally associated with women, a powerful and elemental symbol of connection (Elsley 9)

4.3.3.4. Naming

Names in the novel are chosen in a matrilinieal manner that "reflects Walker's literary and family debt". (Joannau 179) The name Shug is not only a name that occurs in a Zora Neale Hurston novel but was also the name of her grandfather's lover. The name Sofia derive from the Goddess of wisdom. Olivia is out of a novel by Virginia Woolf and Celie's sister Nettie got her name from Walker's maternal grandmother. (see Joannau 179)

4.3.3.5. Quilting

Sewing a quilt is a Northern American tradition, a tradition carried out by women. Celie sews quilts, she takes small pattern of fabric, tears clothes and garments apart to start fresh, to create something new. A patchwork quilt can not come into being without the process of tearing. (see Elsley 4) Thinking of the novel it works like a quilt, many little pieces come together to form a bigger one. Even Celie can be read like a quilt, throughout the story she is torn apart but is still able to bring all the pieces together to form a new, beautiful, improved self.

Through quilting Sofia and Celie define their friendship new. After Celie suggested that Harpo should beat her, Sofia brings Celie her curtains back, the two talk with each other in an honest way and as a peace agreement Sofia offers to make quilt "out of those messed up curtains". (Purple 41)

> Me and Sofia work on the quilt. Got it frame up on the porch. Shug Avery donate her old yellow dress for scrap, and I work in a piece every chance I get. It a nice pattern called Sister's Choice. (Purple 56)

Sister's Choice is not only a traditional pattern moreover it stands for the renewal of the relationship between Celie and Sofia. The quilt is a sign for their revived and bloomed sisterhood. (see Elsley 9) Another pattern used in the book is the simple 9-patch pattern. Again it is used at a time when two female characters start to argue. On her dying bed Corrine gets very jealous of Nettie, who she thinks to be the mother of "her" children.

Nettie is only able to convince her of the opposite by showing her a quilt that Corrina made using the fabric that she had bought when she had met Celie. It is that quilt that reminds Corrina of Celie and the resemblance that she had with her children. It not only affects the then reconstructed friendship between Nettie and Corrine but also "reunites Celie with her babies" (see Elsley 14) by pronouncing her the mother of the children.

4.4. Setting

The story is set near Eatonton, Georgia, the area where Alice Walker grew up. As no historic dates are given it is hard to precisely name an exact date but it is very likable that the story takes place in the early 20th century covering a time span of about 40 years. (see Joannou 175; Bates 90)

4.5. Narrative Techniques

The book is an epistolary novel. In 51 letters Celie writes to god about her life using writing to free herself. The rest is somehow a partly unanswered "correspondence" between Celie and Nettie. (see Bates 90-92) The form of the epistolary novel makes it possible to view the story from different point of views. It is somehow ironic that Walker chose that form of narrative as the early epistolary novels were mainly written by men in the 18th century and initially meant the "preserve of privileged, middle class young ladies" (Joannau 176-177)

Throughout the story words, and language in generally, create authenticity. Celie writes her letters in a form of early African American Vernacular. Nettie on the other side writes her letters in a more educated manner as the following two examples clearly state.

> Letter by Celie: "Us give her a old pocketbook look like a quilt and a little black bible." (Purple 87)
> Letter by Nettie: "I woke up this morning bound to tell Corrine and Samuel everything." (Purple 166)

While Celie uses the simple grammatical structure she is used to, Nettie not only uses an appropriate grammar but also shows her ability to vary her choice of vocabulary. Both types of letter function as mirrors of the writers education and writing abilities.

Both letters are written in 1st person narrator which besides the use of authenticity creates a closer relationship to the reader.

The Color Purple is also often referred to as "modern day slave narrative". Slave narratives were revolutionary texts at their time, making it possible for oppressed people to tell the burden of their life and through this liberate themselves as well as presenting the cruelties they had to suffer. (see Hooks 193-223) Through her novel, Walker reminds us that the days of slavery, although they had officially ended, have not ended for some people at that time and even nowadays the reader is sadly reminded ot the ongoing burden of slavery in this world. Men and women are still oppressed and that even though the Civil Right Movement fought for equal rights, a struggle throughout which women often were excluded and not treated equally.

5. Conclusion

Alice Walker's *The Color Purple* is a text of utmost complexity that makes a coverage of all the important topics talked about sheer impossible. The text has been analysed many times by a vast number of different authors as well as Walker herself. This paper tried to set the novel in context with different aspects of the authors life as well as the sociocultural aspects of the timespan covered in the novel as well as by Alice Walker's life. A clear focus was put on motifs, themes and symbolism throughout the story, focusing only on a few, by far not covering all of them, still giving an introduction to the topic.

6. Bibliography

Bates, Gerri. Alice Walker: A Critical Companion. Westport: Greenwood Press, 2005. 1-51; 88-102

Berlant, Lauren. "Race, Gender and Nation". Alice Walker. Ed. Henry Louis Gates, Jr. and K. A. Appiah. New York: Amistad Press, Inc., 1993. 211-239.

Bobo, Jaqueline. Black Women as Cultural Readers. New York: Columbia University Press, 1995. 60-132.

Christian, Barbara. "Novels for Everyday Use". *Alice Walker*. Ed. Henry Louis Gates, Jr. and K. A. Appiah. New York: Amistad Press, Inc., 1993. 50-105.

Collins, Patricia Hill. Black Feminist Thought. New York: Routledge, 2000. 42, 43, 104, 105, 118, 119, 145-157.

Dillman, Caroline Matheny. Southern Women. New York: Hemisphere Publ., 1988

Elsley, Judy. Quilts as Text(iles): The Semiotics of Quilting. New York: Peter Lang Publishing, Inc., 1996. 1-19.

Erickson, Peter. "Cast Out Alone / to Heal / and Re-create / Ourselves: Family-Based Identity in the Work of Alice Walker". *Alice Walker*. Ed. Harold Bloom. New York: Chelses House Publishers, 1989. 5-25.

Ferber, Michael. A Dictionary of Literary Symbols. 2nd ed. Cambridge: Cambridge University Press, 2007.

Hooks, Bell. "Reading and Resistance: The Color Purple". *Alice Walker*. Ed. Henry Louis Gates, Jr. and K. A. Appiah. New York: Amistad Press, Inc., 1993. 284-296.

Joannou, Maroula. Contemporary Women's Writing. Manchester: Manchester University Press, 2000. 164-185.

Johnson, Yvonne. The Voices of African American Women: The Use of Narrative and Authorial Voice in the Works of Harriet Jacobs, Zora Neale Hurston, and Alice Walker. New York: Peter Lang Publishing, Inc., 1998, 1999. 79-111.

Walker, Alice: In Love and Trouble. New York: Harcourt Brace Jovanovich, 1973.

Walker, Alice. In Search of Our Mothers' Gardens. San Diego, Calif, 1983.

Walker, Alice. The Color Purple. 1983. London: Orion Books Ltd., 2004.

Walker, Alice. The Same River Twice. New York: Scribner, 1996.

Walker, Alice. The Way Forward is with a Broken Heart. London, Women Press, 2001.

Wilson, Charles Reagan. Myth, Manners and Memory. The New Encyclopedia of

Southern Culture 4. North Carolina: The University of North Carolina Press, 2006.

Winchell, Donna Haisty. Alice Walker. New York: Macmillan Publishing Company, 1992. 84-99.

Lightning Source UK Ltd.
Milton Keynes UK
UKRC01n0316080917
308789UK00001B/1